REVEALING
THE PLAN OF SALVATION
IN THE NARRATIVE
OF THE
BOOK
OF
MORMON

A SCRIPTURE PATTERN
TO ENHANCE YOUR STUDY

CAMERON REID ARMSTRONG

Pimpernel Press
Provo, Utah

©2024 by Cameron Reid Armstrong. All rights reserved.
Printed in the United States of America. No portion of this publication may be reproduced or used in any manner without written consent.

Cameron Reid Armstrong
Pimpernel Press 2024

Names: Armstrong, Cameron Reid, Author.

Title: Revealing the Plan of Salvation in the Narrative of The Book of Mormon: A Scripture Pattern to Enhance Your Study

Description: Provo, Utah: Pimpernel Press, [2024]

> Summary: "Learn how the Book of Mormon is filled with illustrations that reveal the plan of salvation through types and shadows in the narrative of events and not just through the discourses. Using this scriptural pattern, the reader will appreciate not only the grandeur of the Book of Mormon but also why it is important to read the other sacred texts and study the teachings of modern-day prophets."

Cover Design: Cameron Reid Armstrong
Photo: Brian Walker

ISBN # 979-8-9879812-2-1 (Paperback)

First Edition 2024

This material is neither made, provided, approved, nor endorsed by Intellectual Reserve, Inc. or The Church of Jesus Christ of Latter-day Saints. Any content or opinions expressed, implied or included in or with the material are solely those of the owner and not those of Intellectual Reserve, Inc. or The Church of Jesus Christ of Latter-day Saints.

Copyrited Material

To Elder Christian Barlow

*The missionary companion who taught me how to ponder.
He helped to find this pattern.*

CONTENTS

    Acknowledgments I

    Preface III

Chapter 1 Revealing the Plan of Salvation 1

Chapter 2 Parables, Tyles, and Shadows. 11

Chapter 3 This Pattern Testifies of Jesus Christ 21

Chapter 4 Mortal Life: Defending and Protecting Our Homes. 35

Chapter 5 See Yourself in The Plan 39

Chapter 6 The Plan of Salvation is a Key to Conversion 45

    References 49

    About the Author 55

    Other Books by Cameron Reid Armstrong 56

ACKNOWLEDGMENTS

Have you ever had a tradition with a friend that lasted years? My friend Brian Walker and I worked at the same place for ten years; most Fridays we would talk and decompress in my office, or his classroom. Brian and I were given the same spirit guide, so we deemed these gatherings "Fox Talk."

During one of these talks, I shared my thoughts on the plan of salvation being revealed in the narratives in the Book of Mormon, and I received a very different response from Brian than from others with whom I'd shared this. Most family and friends had positive and excited reactions--Brian told me to write a book. A few weeks later Brian followed up about the book idea. When I responded that I had done nothing with his request, he stood at the whiteboard to help brainstorm the concepts and outline the chapters.

A few months ago, I felt stuck in my progress, and--without me asking--Brian was there again. During Brian's layover in the Denver, Colorado airport, he called me to check in, and we eventually set a deadline and established the motivation to keep it. After that call, Brian shared with me many weeknights with Thai food and Saturday mornings with breakfast burritos going over the manuscript and giving feedback. Brian is why this book was conceived, written, and finished. (He also took my photo for the back of the book.)

Brian, I can't thank you enough for your friendship.

My writing group's support and feedback for this project helped tremendously. Another tradition, that has continued on the second Saturday of every month, for years. Thank you, my friends, The Breakfast Club: Irene Bolter, Brady Clegg, Sam Coates, Nathan Sellers, and, of course, Brian Walker.

I also can't forget the patience of my wife and kids as I have worked on this project.

"God bless us all to use all the scriptures, but in particular the instrument He designed to bring us to Christ—the Book of Mormon."
- Ezra Taft Benson

PREFACE

For members of the Church of Jesus Christ of Latter-Day Saints, daily scripture study can occasionally be a complicated task. There are numerous sacred texts to choose from: The Bible, Book of Mormon, Doctrine and Covenants, Pearl of Great Price, and then every six months a new set of general conference addresses comes out. The demands of each member's time can feel like a cup that runneth over.

This book is a call to focus on the Book of Mormon. It also offers strong encouragement to study all the books of scripture. As you study, let your mind ponder on one constant topic: the plan of salvation. Joseph Smith spoke on the importance of studying the plan of salvation; he said, "The great plan of salvation is a theme which ought to occupy our strict attention, and be regarded as one of heaven's best gifts to mankind… and it is a subject we ought to study more than any other. We ought to study it day and night, for the world is ignorant in reference to their true condition and relation [to God]."[2]

While this book won't provide a comprehensive outlook on the plan of salvation, it hopes to be an introduction to a scriptural pattern that helps the reader learn the plan of salvation. President Benson once asked, "Are we using the messages and the method of teaching found in the Book of Mormon and other scriptures of the Restoration to teach this great plan of the Eternal God?"[3] This book introduces a pattern you can include in your study and preparation for talks or lessons.

The book was written by a layman for all laymen who desire to be consistent in their scripture study. This method of study shows how consistent reading and pondering can be fun, engaging, and can bless you for many years. The author recommends seeking a balance between exegesis[1] and eisegesis[2] when interpreting scripture, always relying on the Spirit of Truth.

---

1 Exegesis: A way of interpreting scripture that lets the meaning come from the text itself.
2 Eisegesis: A way of interpreting scripture that the reader brings meaning to the text.

> *"God's plan, however, is not something to be deduced by logic alone, nor is human experience deep enough or long enough to inform us adequately. It requires revelation from God."*
> − NEIL A MAXWELL

1

REVEALING THE PLAN OF SALVATION

Have you ever read a book more than once? Was it a book that was fun and exciting or one that was more difficult to understand? People tend to avoid reading lengthy books that are confusing to them. Have the scriptures become like this to you? You may have expressed a familiar groan from past studies as you approach the task of reading the scriptures. "Ugh, you want me to read this book every day?" "I've already read it; why should I reread it? I don't even understand a lot of what is written anyway." These are understandable questions. However, remember the teacher who made that stuffy old book come alive? Somehow that story became a classic to you as well. You came to love the layered meanings that were invisible before that teacher helped reveal them to you.

The Bible Dictionary defines a mystery as "a spiritual truth that was once hidden but now is revealed and that without special revelation would have remained unknown." (see Bible Dictionary, Mystery p.736) Paul's words often come to mind when I think about the purpose of consistent scripture study: "Eye hath not seen, nor ear heard, neither have entered into the heart of man, the things which God hath prepared for them that love him" (see 1 Corinthians 2:9–12). The scriptural pattern introduced in this book can enhance your scripture study and help you recognize the layered meanings that were once unseen, helping you enjoy the Book of Mormon over and over again.

A Mysterious Question in the Book of Jarom

The second verse in the book of Jarom includes a question that can change the way you approach your study of the Book of Mormon:

> And as these plates are small, and as these things are written for the intent of the benefit of our brethren the Lamanites, wherefore, it must needs be that I write a little; but I shall not write the things of my prophesying, nor of my revelations. For what could I write more than my fathers have written? *For have not they revealed the plan of salvation?* I say unto you, Yea; and this sufficeth me. (Jarom 1:2; emphasis added).

In Jarom's view, his fathers—as recorded in 1 Nephi through Enos—had already revealed the plan of salvation! This sparks another question: "Where is the plan of salvation revealed in the Book of Mormon?" A keen student can identify places where the plan was taught, such as Lehi teaching his sons in 2 Nephi 2:14-29. However, examples like that demonstrate how the plan is preached and discussed, but not revealed. Jarom's use of the word "revealed" ought to stand out in your mind and be the catalyst for other questions:

- Does Jarom mean the plan of salvation was revealed in its entirety?
- What parts of the plan might be missing from the text? What about the premortal council or the War in Heaven?
- What about the gospel being preached to the dead in spirit prison? Where does the Book of Mormon teach about that part of the plan of salvation?

Keep these questions in mind as you walk through the following exercise. By searching for how the plan of salvation is revealed in the narrative of the Book of Mormon, you can gain additional insights from your study.

A Mystery in the Book of Helaman

The scriptural account in the first chapter of the book of Helaman describes an event that seems fundamentally historical. It outlines a contentious political struggle during the election of a new Nephite chief judge. There is no explicit mention of Jesus Christ, His gospel, or anything that seems to merit its inclusion on the plates. Ask yourself, "If Mormon didn't have much room on the plates, why include this event in the Book of Mormon?" Mormon described his process of selecting what he included from the Nephite record: "I do not know all things; but the Lord knoweth all things...wherefore, he worketh in me to do according to his will" (see Words of Mormon 1:7).

Take a minute to think about the plan of salvation before you read the first chapter of Helaman. Specifically note these points about our premortal existence and the War in Heaven.

The council in heaven (see Abraham 3:22-28; D&C 29:36-37)
- All of God's children were present.
- The plan was introduced (go down to earth, follow the commandments, be redeemed).
- Two sons volunteered to be the Son of God and redeem mankind.
- Agency was given to choose between the two who volunteered.

Jehovah (see Abraham 3:27; Revelation 13:8)
- He was chosen to be our Redeemer.
- He is the Lamb slain from the foundation of the world.

Lucifer/The Devil/Satan (see Abraham 3:27-28; D&C 29:36-37)
- He coveted God's power.
- He was angry for not being chosen.
- He rebelled.
- He was recruiting/flattering/deceiving his followers.
- He was cast out of God's presence to Earth (separation from God is spiritual death).

God's children at war (see Revelation 12:4,7-11; Moses 4:3; D&C 29:36-37)
- Two-thirds part of God's spirit children chose to follow Jehovah.
- A third part chose Lucifer (they became the devil and his angels).

Lucifer and his angels were cast out of heaven (see D&C 29:36-39)
- They came to earth as disembodied spirts (separation from God is spiritual death).
- They tempt us to disobey as we learn good from evil.

Now that you have pondered these facets of our premortal existence and the War in Heaven, continue with this experiment by reading Helaman 1:1-12. If you prefer, you can use the Book of Mormon text included to mark down your own thoughts as you read.

THE BOOK OF HELAMAN

An account of the Nephites. Their wars and contentions, and their dissensions. And also the prophecies of many holy prophets, before the coming of Christ, according to the records of Helaman, who was the son of Helaman, and also according to the records of his sons, even down to the coming of Christ. And also many of the Lamanites are converted. An account of their conversion. An account of the righteousness of the Lamanites, and the wickedness and abominations of the Nephites, according to the record of Helaman and his sons, even down to the coming of Christ, which is called the book of Helaman, and so forth.

CHAPTER 1

Pahoran the second becomes chief judge and is murdered by Kishkumen—Pacumeni fills the judgment seat—Coriantumr leads the Lamanite armies, takes Zarahemla, and slays Pacumeni—Moronihah defeats the Lamanites and retakes Zarahemla, and Coriantumr is slain. About 52–50 B.C.

1 And now behold, it came to pass in the commencement of the fortieth year of the reign of the judges over the people of Nephi, there began to be a serious difficulty among the people of the Nephites.

2 For behold, Pahoran had died, and gone the way of all the earth; therefore there began to be a serious contention concerning who should have the judgment-seat among the brethren, who were the sons of Pahoran.

3 Now these are their names who did contend for the judgment-seat, who did also cause the people to contend: Pahoran, Paanchi, and Pacumeni.

4 Now these are not all the sons of Pahoran (for he had many), but these are they who did contend for the judgment-seat; therefore, they did cause three divisions among the people.

5 Nevertheless, it came to pass that Pahoran was appointed by the voice of the people to be chief judge and a governor over the people of Nephi.

6 And it came to pass that Pacumeni, when he saw that he could not obtain the judgment-seat, he did unite with the voice of the people.

7 But behold, Paanchi, and that part of the people that were desirous that he should be their governor, was exceedingly wroth;

therefore, he was about to flatter away those people to rise up in rebellion against their brethren.

8 And it came to pass as he was about to do this, behold, he was taken, and was tried according to the voice of the people, and condemned unto death; for he had raised up in rebellion and sought to destroy the liberty of the people.

9 Now when those people who were desirous that he should be their governor saw that he was condemned unto death, therefore they were angry, and behold, they sent forth one Kishkumen, even to the judgment-seat of Pahoran, and murdered Pahoran as he sat upon the judgment-seat.

10 And he was pursued by the servants of Pahoran; but behold, so speedy was the flight of Kishkumen that no man could overtake him.

11 And he went unto those that sent him, and they all entered into a covenant, yea, swearing by their everlasting Maker, that they would tell no man that Kishkumen had murdered Pahoran.

12 Therefore, Kishkumen was not known among the people of Nephi, for he was in disguise at the time that he murdered Pahoran. And Kishkumen and his band, who had covenanted with him, did mingle themselves among the people, in a manner that they all could not be found; but as many as were found were condemned unto death.

The Plan of Salvation is Revealed
Through the Narrative of the Events

As you read about this political struggle, do you see similarities between our premortal life and this chapter in the Book of Mormon? Perhaps the inspired writers and compilers of the Book of Mormon chose specific events from their history to be used as types and shadows to teach us about the plan of salvation. Below are some of the "mysteries" revealed in these verses that you may have noticed.

THE BOOK OF HELAMAN

CHAPTER 1

Pahoran the second becomes chief judge and is murdered by Kishkumen—Pacumeni fills the judgment seat—Coriantumr leads the Lamanite armies, takes Zarahemla, and slays Pacumeni—Moronihah defeats the Lamanites and retakes Zarahemla, and Coriantumr is slain. About 52–50 B.C.

1 And now behold, it came to pass in the commencement of the fortieth year of the reign of the judges over the people of Nephi, there began to be **a serious difficulty among the people** of the Nephites.
2 For behold, Pahoran had died, and gone the way of all the earth; therefore there began to be a **serious contention concerning who should have the judgment-seat** among the brethren, who were the sons of Pahoran.
3 Now these are their names **who did contend for the judgment-seat**, who did also cause the people to contend: Pahoran, Paanchi, and Pacumeni.
4 Now these are **not all the sons** of Pahoran (**for he had many**), but these are they who did contend for the judgment-seat; therefore, **they did cause three divisions** among the people.
5 Nevertheless, it came to pass that Pahoran was **appointed by the voice of the people** to be **chief judge** and a **governor** over the people of Nephi.
6 And it came to pass that **Pacumeni**, when he saw that he could not obtain the judgment-seat, **he did unite with the voice of the people**.
7 But behold, Paanchi, and that part of the people that were desirous that he should be their governor, **was exceedingly wroth**;

Handwritten annotations:

- GOD HAS MANY CHILDREN "ONE SAID, 'SEND ME'"
- PEOPLE DIVIDED INTO THREE PARTS — PAHORAN 1/3, PAANCHI 1/3, PACUMENI 1/3
- PAHORAN JR — SAME NAME AS HIS FATHER — FIRSTBORN? — APPOINTED BY THE VOICE OF THE PEOPLE
- AGENCY
- PAHORAN'S PART + PACUMENI'S PART = 2/3 PART OF THE PEOPLE CHOOSE PAHORAN
- WAR OVER WHO SHOULD BE CHOSEN
- MORMON 3:20 STAND BEFORE THE JUDGEMENT-SEAT OF CHRIST
- ABRAHAM 3:27 "WHOM SHALL I SEND?" ONE SAID, "SEND ME" ANOTHER SAID, "SEND ME"
- "I WILL SEND THE FIRST" — MENTIONED FIRST
- MENTIONED SECOND
- THIRD
- ABRAHAM 3:28 THE SECOND WAS ANGRY

6

369　　　　　　　　　　　　　　　　　　　　Helaman 1:8-12

PAANCHI'S 1/3 PART

REVELATION 12:4, 7-11; D&C 29:36
THE DEVIL... REBELLED
A THIRD PART OF THE HOSTS
OF HEAVEN TURNED HE AWAY

therefore, he was about to **flatter away those people** to **rise up in rebellion** against their brethren.

8 And it came to pass as he was about to do this, behold, he was **taken**, and was **tried** according to the voice of the people, and **condemned unto death**; for he had raised up in rebellion and **sought to destroy the liberty of the people**.

9 Now when those people who were desirous that he should be their governor saw that he was condemned unto death, therefore **they were angry**, and behold, they sent forth one Kishkumen, even to the judgment-seat of Pahoran, and murdered Pahoran as he sat **upon the judgment-seat**.

10 And he was pursued by the servants of Pahoran; but behold, so speedy was the flight of Kishkumen that no man could overtake him.

11 And he went unto those that sent him, **and they all entered into a covenant**, yea, **swearing by their everlasting Maker**, that they would tell no man that Kishkumen had murdered Pahoran.

12 Therefore, Kishkumen was not known among the people of Nephi, for he was **in disguise** at the time that he murdered Pahoran. And Kishkumen and his band, who had covenanted with him, **did mingle themselves among the people**, in a manner that they all could not be found; but as **many** as were found **were condemned unto death**.

PAANCHI'S PHYSICAL DEATH
LUCIFER'S SPIRITUAL DEATH
ABRAHAM 3:28
KEPT NOT HIS FIRST ESTATE
MANY FOLLOWED AFTER HIM

MOSES 4:3
SATAN... SOUGHT TO DESTROY
THE AGENCY OF MAN

REVELATION 13:8
THE LAMB SLAIN
FROM THE FOUNDATION
OF THE WORLD

3 NEPHI 27:14
UPON THE CROSS

D&C 29:37
THEY WERE THRUST DOWN
THUS BECAME THE DEVIL
AND HIS ANGELS

PHYSICAL DEATH OF
PAANCHI'S FOLLOWERS
=
SPIRITUAL DEATH OF
LUCIFER'S FOLLOWERS

7

With this scriptural pattern, you can use keywords or concepts found in a Book of Mormon event that are also used in other parts of scripture that teach about the plan of salvation. These similar words can cue your thoughts and help you ponder additional connections. For example, Helaman 1:3 describes a contention for a judgment seat. Other scriptures teach that the judgment seat was eventually occupied by Jesus Christ.

Heleman 1:3	Keywords From Both Scriptures		Mormon 3:20
3 Now these are their names who did contend for the judgment-seat, who did also cause the people to contend: Pahoran, Paanchi, and Pacumeni.	The judgment-seat	The judgment-seat	20 ... all stand before the judgment-seat of Christ, yea, every soul who belongs to the whole human family of Adam

Using this approach, your mind may call up other questions or thoughts, such as, "What about the death of Pahoran's son?" "Is this a type of Christ?" "Pahoran is dead and no longer has any power or influence." As you study Jehovah's role in the premortal realm, this quote from LeGrand Richards can offer an additional insight into Christ's death: "We read of Christ, the Lamb slain before the foundation of this earth. Not that He was literally slain, but in the Lord's great eternal plan, He had offered Himself and He was to give His life."[28]

Heleman 1:9	Keywords From Both Scriptures		3 Nephi 27:14
9 ...Kishkumen... murdered Pahoran as he sat upon the judgment-seat.	Upon the judgement seat	Upon the cross	14 And my Father sent me that I might be lifted up upon the cross...

This scriptural pattern helps the Book of Mormon become, as Alma promises, a seed that will begin to "swell within your [breast]... and "enlighten [your] understanding." Extracting insights from the narrative of Book of Mormon events will become "delicious to [you]" as you study with this new perspective (see Alma 32:28).

The Book of Mormon truly does contain "the fulness of [the] everlasting gospel." (see D&C 27:5) Read on for additional guidance on how to have the plan of salvation revealed to you from the narrative of the Book of Mormon.

*"To the dull and uninspired it is a mere story, 'seeing they see not,'
while to the instructed and spiritual it reveals the mysteries
or secrets of the kingdom of heaven."*
- Bible Dictionary: Parable

2

PARABLES, TYPES, AND SHADOWS

As Jesus' fame grew, so did His audience. This large audience included people with different intentions. Some wanted to follow Him as their Savior. Some wanted to trick or trap Him. Some wanted healing. Some wanted a political figure. Some wanted to be spiritually fed while some were most interested in being physically fed. Considering these differences in intentions, Jesus, to the surprise of everyone, began to teach in parables. Even His apostles were confused and asked, "Why speakest thou in parables?" Jesus answered, "For you it is given to know the mysteries of the kingdom, for them they are not to know" (see Matthew 13:10-11).

Similarly, the Book of Mormon now has a worldwide audience of readership. People study and read with various intentions. The Lord in His wisdom hid many truths in the accounts included in the Book of Mormon. These truths can be revealed to those who hath ears to hear or eyes to see.

The events in the Book of Mormon are not identified by the authors as parables. They are real accounts of an ancient people, yet they can be studied in the same way as a parable. The Bible Dictionary defines the technique: "The word parable is Greek in origin and means a setting side by side, a comparison. In parables divine truth is presented by comparison with material things." (Bible Dictionary: Parable)

Parables often use figurative language. Jesus would teach divine truth by saying that "The kingdom of heaven is like…" and then use relatable physical objects or events as types and shadows that teach gospel principles through symbolism. For example: "a grain of mustard seed," "a treasure hid in a field," "a net cast into the sea" (see Matthew 13:31-32,44, 47).

Consider reading the Book of Mormon accounts with a comparable lens: "Our premortal existence with a War in Heaven is like...an election of a chief judge" (see Helaman 1:1-12).

The Bible Dictionary suggests not only how to study parables but also how one can understand them. It reads:

> The parable conveys to the hearer religious truth exactly in proportion to his faith and intelligence; to the dull and uninspired it is a mere story, "seeing they see not," while to the instructed and spiritual it reveals the mysteries or secrets of the kingdom of heaven. (Bible Dictionary: Parable)

As you continue your scripture study, look for words that stand out as unique, oddly used, or repeated often. Pondering these words can give you eyes to see and ears to hear. As you are consistent in your study, the Lord will bring these keywords back to your remembrance[6], and the events can take on additional meaning as parables that reveal His plan through types and shadows.

Side-by-Side Comparisons of Keywords: Nephi and Zeniff

Keywords can be found throughout the scriptures or other authorized prophetic teachings where the plan of salvation is discussed. One such example comes from Joseph Smith's King Follett Sermon. In this sermon, Joseph Smith presents a key concept about the creation of the Earth. His phrasing can help identify how Nephi reveals the plan of salvation. Joseph Smith said, "Now, the word create came from the word baurau which does not mean to create out of nothing; it means to organize; the same as a man would organize materials and build a ship."[7] Just as God created the Earth with elements He already had, Nephi built a ship using elements already available in the land of Bountiful. Under the Lord's direction, Lehi's family organized ore and timber and other materials to construct a ship.

Try another experiment; see how Nephi's writings revealed how the creation of the earth is like building a ship. The comparison of keywords in both narratives gives testimony to Alma's statement: "The scriptures are laid before thee, yea, and all things denote there is a God" (Alma 30:44). Even the process of building a boat can instruct us in God's plan.

1 Nephi 8,17-18: The Creation of the Earth is Like Nephi Building a Ship

Read these passages, ponder them, and identify possible keywords that relate to a portion of the plan of salvation—the Creation.

1 Nephi 8:1   1 Nephi 17:4,6,8,10,36   1 Nephi 18:1-2,4-6, 8
Genesis 1:10, 12   Abraham 3:24
Dallin H. Oaks, "The Great Plan of Happiness", Ensign, Nov 1993

As you study these passages, it can be helpful to line them up in a side-by-side comparison with Nephi's inspired account. Can you see how Nephi reveals important insights into the creation of the Earth? Use the chart, and build upon the insights already included.

Nephite Event	Keywords		Creation Event
Construction of the Ship	In order, as they appear in the text:	Lined up with corresponding keywords:	**Creation of the Earth**
1 Nephi 17:4,6 4 And we did <u>sojourn</u>... even <u>eight years in the wilderness.</u> 6 And it came to pass that we did <u>pitch our tents by the seashore</u>	- Sojourn eight years in the wilderness - pitched our tents by the seashore	"We had progressed as far as we could (without a physical body and an experience in mortality)."	**Dallin H. Oaks, "The Great Plan of Happiness", Ensign, Nov 1993** "Our understanding of life begins with a council in heaven... <u>We had progressed as far as we could without a physical body and an experience in mortality.</u>"
1 Nephi 17:8,10 8 ...Thou shalt <u>construct a ship</u>... <u>that I may carry thy people across these waters.</u> 10 ...the Lord told me whither I should go to <u>find ore,</u> that I might <u>make tools</u>.	- Construct a ship - That I may carry thy people across these waters - Find ore, make tools	- we will take of these materials, and we will make an earth	
1 Nephi 17:36 36 Behold, the Lord hath <u>created the earth</u> that it should be inhabited... <u>created his children that they should possess it.</u>	- Created the earth - Created his children that they should possess it	- Whereon these may dwell	**Abraham 3:24** ...We will <u>go down</u>, for there is space there, and <u>we will take of these materials, and we will make an earth whereon these may dwell;</u>
1 Nephi 18:1-2,4 1 ...we did <u>work timbers of curious workmanship.</u> 2 Now I, Nephi, did... <u>work the timbers</u>... 4 <u>I had finished the ship</u>... my brethren <u>beheld that it was good</u>...	- Work timbers of curious workmanship - Work the timbers - I had finished the ship - Beheld that it was good	- Organize; the same as a man would organize materials and build a ship - -	**Joseph Smith, The King Follett Sermon** "Now, the word create came from the word baurau... it means to <u>organize; the same as a man would organize materials and build a ship.</u>"
1 Nephi 18:5-6 5 And... the voice of the Lord... arise and <u>go down into the ship</u>. 6 ... after we had prepared all things, much <u>fruits</u>... we did <u>go down into the ship,</u> with all our loading and our <u>seeds,</u> ... wherefore, we did all <u>go down into the ship, with our wives and our children.</u>	- Go down into the ship - Fruits - Go down into the ship - Seeds - Go down into the ship, with our wives and our children	- Go down - - - -	**Genesis 1:10,12** 10 And God called the dry land Earth... and God saw that it was good. 12 And the earth brought forth grass, and herb yielding seed after his kind, and the tree yielding fruit, whose seed was in itself, after his kind: and God saw that it was good.
1 Nephi 18:8 8 And it came to pass after we had all <u>gone down into the ship,</u> and had taken <u>with</u> us <u>our provisions</u> (Provisions are described in **1 Nephi 8:1** 1 And it came to pass that we had gathered together all manner of <u>seeds of every kind,</u> both of <u>grain of every kind,</u> and also of the seeds of <u>fruit of every kind.</u>)	- Gone down into the ship... with... our provisions - Seeds of every kind - Grain of every kind - Seeds of fruit of every kind	- - - -	

Mosiah 9-10: The Creation and The Fall is Like Zeniff Establishing the Land of Nephi

Read these passages, ponder them, and identify possible keywords that relate to the plan of salvation—the Creation and the Fall:

Mosiah 9:6-9   Mosiah 9:5,10-11   Mosiah 10:3-5   Genesis 1:28
Genesis 2:5   Genesis 3:6-7   2 Nephi 28:19,21-22

An event contained in the book of Mosiah shows the establishment of the land of Nephi. Similar to Nephi building a ship, Zeniff and his people built their homes out of materials that were already there. Joseph Smith's address gave us the key concept to look for, and a similar concept was also taught by President Russell M. Nelson. Speaking of the newly constructed conference center at the time, he exclaimed:

> The process of construction is truly inspiring to me. From conception to completion, any major building project reflects upon the work of the Master Creator. In fact, the Creation—of planet Earth and of life upon it—undergirds all other creative capability. Any manmade creation is possible only because of our divine Creator. The people who design and build are given life and capacity by that Creator. And all materials used in the construction of an edifice are ultimately derived from the rich resources of the earth... Grand as it is, planet Earth is part of something even grander—that great plan of God. Simply summarized, the earth was created that families might be.[22]

The people of Zeniff are in transition from Zarahemla to the land of Nephi. The king of the Lamanites, with the hope of bringing them into bondage, allows Zeniff's people to take occupancy of the land. As you read about this interaction, you may see keywords from Genesis 1:28 and Genesis 2:5 that go along with President Russell M. Nelson's quote. These events reveal insights into the creation.

MOSIAH 9:6-9

GENESIS 1:28 — SUBDUE IT; AND HAVE DOMINION

RUSSELL M. NELSON — THE CREATION OF PLANET EARTH... UNDERGIRDS ALL OTHER CREATIVE CAPABILITY... THE PEOPLE WHO DESIGN AND BUILD ARE GIVEN LIFE AND CAPACITY BY THAT CREATOR.

GENESIS 2:5 — EVERY PLANT OF THE FIELD — EVERY HERB OF THE FIELD — TILL THE GROUND

GENESIS 1:28 — BE FRUITFUL, AND MULTIPLY, AND REPLENISH THE EARTH

6 And I went in unto the king, and **he covenanted with me that I might possess the land** of Lehi-Nephi, and the land of Shilom.
7 And he also commanded that his people should depart out of the land, and I and my people went into the land that we might possess it.
8 And we began to **build buildings, and to repair The walls** of the city, yea, even the walls of the city of Lehi-Nephi, and the city of Shilom.
9 And **we began to till the ground**, yea, even with **all manner of seeds**, with seeds of corn, and of wheat, and of barley, and with neas, and with sheum, and with seeds of **all manner of fruits**; and **we did begin to multiply and prosper in the land**.

14

Nephite Event	Keywords		Creation Event
Possess the Land, Build, Till the Ground, Multiply	**In order, as they appear in the text:**	**Lined up with corresponding keywords:**	**Have Dominion, Till the Ground, Multiply**
Mosiah 9:6-9 6 And I went in unto the king, and <u>he covenanted with me that I might possess the land</u> of Lehi-Nephi, and the land of Shilom. 7 And he also commanded that his people should depart out of the land, and I and my people went into the land that we might possess it. 8 And we began to <u>build buildings, and to repair the walls</u> of the city, yea, even the walls of the city of Lehi-Nephi, and the city of Shilom. 9 And <u>we began to till the ground</u>, yea, even with <u>all manner of seeds</u>, with seeds of corn, and of wheat, and of barley, and with neas, and with sheum, and with seeds of <u>all manner of fruits</u>; and <u>we did begin to multiply and prosper in the land</u>.	- He covenanted with me that I might possess the land - Build buildings, and to repair the walls - We began to till the ground - All manner of seeds - All manner of fruits - We did begin to multiply and prosper in the land	- Subdue it: and have dominion - The Creation—of planet Earth… undergirds all other creative capability... The people who design and build are given life and capacity by that Creator. - Till the ground - Every herb of the field - Every plant of the field - Be fruitful, and multiply, and replenish the earth	**Genesis 1:28** 28 And God blessed them, and God said unto them, <u>Be fruitful, and multiply, and replenish the earth</u>, and <u>subdue it: and have dominion</u> over the fish of the sea, and over the fowl of the air, and over every living thing that moveth upon the earth. **Russell M. Nelson, "The Creation," Ensign, May 2000** <u>The Creation—of planet Earth… undergirds all other creative capability... The people who design and build are given life and capacity by that Creator.</u> **Genesis 2:5** 5 And <u>every plant of the field</u> before it was in the earth, and <u>every herb of the field</u> before it grew: for the Lord God had not caused it to rain upon the earth, and there was not a man to <u>till the ground</u>.

Transitioning from the creation to the fall, notice the disposition of the Lamanite king and his plan to deceive and bring the Nephites into bondage in Mosiah 9:5,10-11. By comparing similar keywords from multiple scriptures and prophetic teachings, you can gain additional understanding about the disposition of Satan. His true desire is to enslave the children of Adam and Eve. Look for the keywords in 2 Nephi 28:19,21-22 where the Book of Mormon teaches the tactics Satan has always used from the beginning.

MOSIAH 9:5,10-11

2 NEPHI 28:19,21-22
- THE DEVIL
- PACIFY, AND LULL THEM AWAY INTO CARNAL SECURITY

- THE DEVIL WILL GRASP THEM WITH HIS EVERLASTING CHAINS

- TELLETH THEM THERE IS NO HELL; AND HE SAITH UNTO THEM: I AM NO DEVIL

5 And it came to pass that I went again with four of my men into the city, in unto the king, that I might **know of the disposition of the king**, and that I might know if I might go in with my people and possess the land in peace.
10 Now it was **the cunning and the craftiness of king** Laman, **to bring my people into bondage**, that he yielded up the land that we might possess it.
11 Therefore it came to pass, that **after we had dwelt in the land for the space of twelve years** that **king** Laman **began to grow uneasy**, **lest by any means my people should wax strong** in the land, and **that they could not overpower them and bring them into bondage**.

2 NEPHI 28:19,21-22
- ALL IS WELL IN ZION; YEA, ZION PROSPERETH
- THE KINGDOM... MUST SHAKE
- OTHERS HE FLATTERETH AWAY
- THUS THE DEVIL CHEATETH THEIR SOULS

- LEADETH THEM AWAY CAREFULLY DOWN TO HELL
- UNTIL HE GRASPS THEM WITH HIS AWFUL CHAINS

Nephite Event	Keywords		Garden of Eden
The Disposition of The King	**In order, as they appear in the text:**	**Lined up with corresponding keywords:**	**The Disposition of The Devil**
Mosiah 9:5,10-11 5 And it came to pass that I went again with four of my men into the city, in unto the king, that I might know of the disposition of the king, and that I might know if I might go in with my people and possess the land in peace. 10 Now it was the cunning and the craftiness of king Laman, to bring my people into bondage, that he yielded up the land that we might possess it. 11 Therefore it came to pass, that after we had dwelt in the land for the space of twelve years that king Laman began to grow uneasy, lest by any means my people should wax strong in the land, and that they could not overpower them and bring them into bondage.	- Know of the disposition of the king - The cunning and the craftiness of [the] king - To bring my people into bondage - That he yielded up the land that we might possess it - After we had dwelt in the land for the space of twelve years - King... began to grow uneasy - Lest by any means my people should wax strong - That they could not overpower them and bring them into bondage	- The devil - Pacify, and lull them away into carnal security - The devil will grasp them with his everlasting chains - Telleth them there is no hell; and he saith unto them: I am no devil - All is well in Zion; yea, Zion prospereth - The kingdom... must shake - Others he flattereth away - Thus the devil cheateth their souls - Leadeth them away carefully down to hell - Until he grasps them with his awful chains	**2 Nephi 28:19,21-22** 19 For the kingdom of the devil must shake, and they which belong to it must needs be stirred up unto repentance, or the devil will grasp them with his everlasting chains, and they be stirred up to anger, and perish; 21 And others will he pacify, and lull them away into carnal security, that they will say: All is well in Zion; yea, Zion prospereth, all is well—and thus the devil cheateth their souls, and leadeth them away carefully down to hell. 22 And behold, others he flattereth away, and telleth them there is no hell; and he saith unto them: I am no devil, for there is none—and thus he whispereth in their ears, until he grasps them with his awful chains, from whence there is no deliverance.

Continue comparing the keywords. You will find more evidence the fall is being taught through the narrative in Mosiah. This is not a coincidence. In the tenth chapter of Mosiah, the people of Zeniff "inherit the land" and "till the ground." You can identify more keywords related to the Creation and the Fall such as *fruit*, *naked*, and actions like *sewing*. Note how the phrase "the land" is used three times in these verses. This should bring your attention to the Earth—a corresponding part of the plan of salvation.

Nephite Event	Keywords		The Fall of Man
Till the Ground, Fruit, Sew, Nakedness	**In order, as they appear in the text:**	**Lined up with corresponding keywords:**	**Till the Ground, Fruit, Sew, Nakedness**
Mosiah 10:3-5 3 And it came to pass that we did inherit the land of our fathers for many years, yea, for the space of twenty and two years. 4 And I did cause that the men should till the ground, and raise all manner of grain and all manner of fruit of every kind. 5 And I did cause that the women should spin, and toil, and work, and work all manner of fine linen, yea, and cloth of every kind, that we might clothe our nakedness; and thus we did prosper in the land—thus we did have continual peace in the land for the space of twenty and two years.	- The land - Men should till the ground - All manner of grain - All manner of fruit - The women - Should spin, and toil - Work all manner of fine linen... cloth of every kind - That we might clothe our nakedness - The land - The land	- The earth - Man to till the ground - Every plant of the field - Every herb of the field - The tree was good for food - Took of the fruit - The woman - They sewed fig leaves together - Made themselves aprons - They knew that they were naked - The earth - The earth	**Genesis 2:5** 5 And every plant of the field before it was in the earth, and every herb of the field before it grew: for the Lord God had not caused it to rain upon the earth, and there was not a man to till the ground. **Genesis 3:6-7** 6 And when the woman saw that the tree was good for food, and that it was pleasant to the eyes, and a tree to be desired to make one wise, she took of the fruit thereof, and did eat, and gave also unto her husband with her; and he did eat. 7 And the eyes of them both were opened, and they knew that they were naked; and they sewed fig leaves together, and made themselves aprons.

Continue your reading while pondering the plan of salvation. Identify the reasons the Nephites are placed into bondage, the way they are delivered, and their return to the land of Zarahemla. In the city of Zarahemla, both groups are received with joy by the king. Compare the diagrams on the following pages. The events of Mosiah 7-26 become a type and a shadow of the entire plan of salvation.

The Plan of Salvation

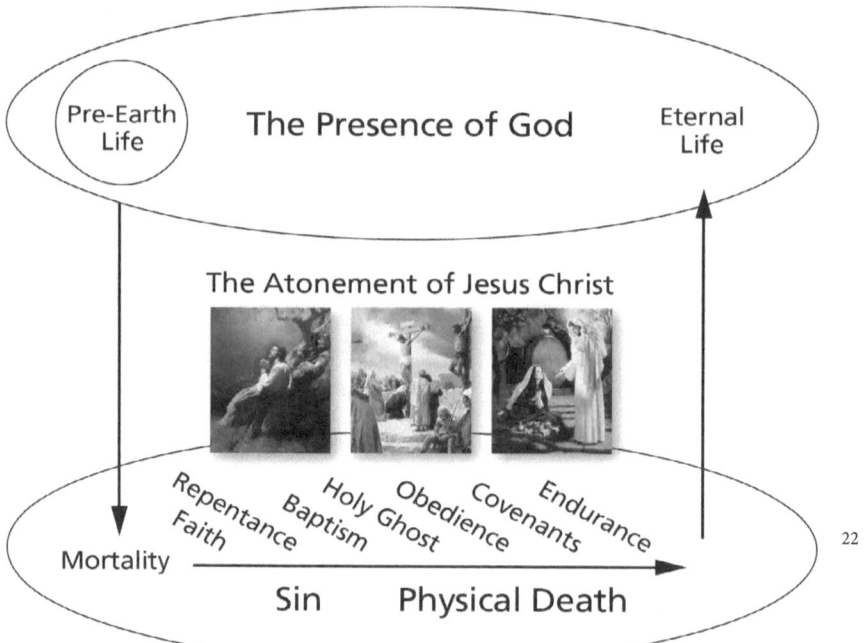

The Journey of Zeniff, Noah/Limhi, and Alma: Mosiah 7-26

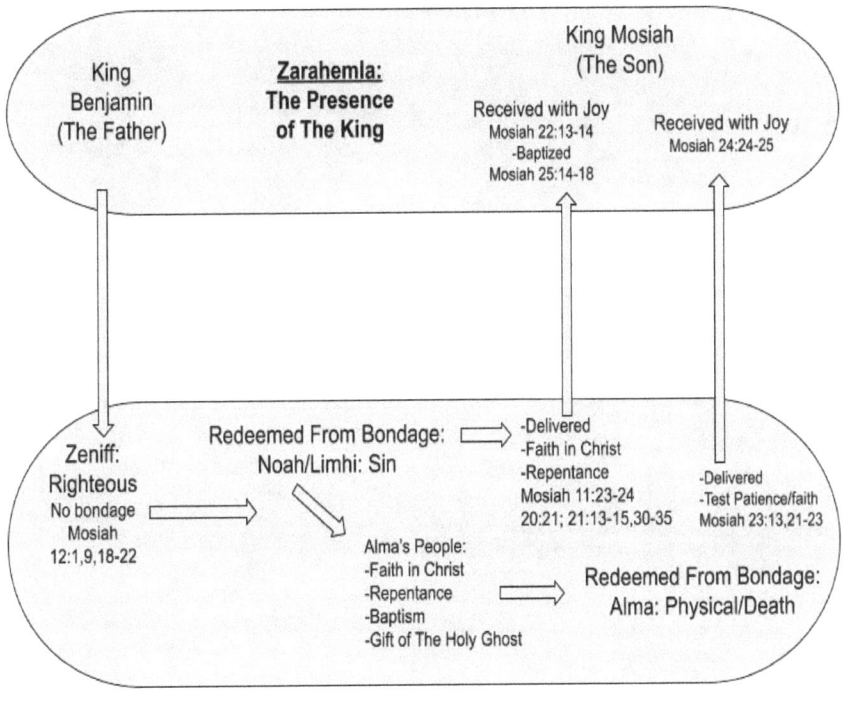

"Few things build faith more than does regular immersion in the Book of Mormon. No other book testifies of Jesus Christ with such power and clarity."
- Russell M. Nelson

3

THIS PATTERN TESTIFIES OF JESUS CHRIST

Have you ever challenged yourself to read the Book of Mormon and mark verses where Christ was mentioned? On average Christ is referenced every 1.7 verses[2]. Sometimes He is mentioned in several verses clustered together, whereas there are other times when whole chapters go by without any explicit mention of Jesus Christ or his Gospel. Approaching your study of the Book of Mormon by searching for elements of God's plan of happiness can help illuminate the implicit references in such chapters. You can start to see types and shadows of Jesus Christ as every page can reveal the plan of salvation.

One event detailed in the 54th and 55th chapters of the book of Alma seems to have little to no references to Christ. In these chapters, Moroni and Ammoron exchange letters discussing the possibility of exchanging prisoners. Upon receiving Ammoron's negative response, Moroni decides instead to use strategy to free his captured people. Through types and shadows, you can see references to Christ in these chapters.

Even with no direct mention of Jesus Christ and His gospel, you can study these wartime narrative events like you would a parable. As you do, you can see that these chapters contain precious insights on justice, mercy, and God's search for a Savior for His children. You will see the Atonement of Christ manifested as His atoning blood satisfies the demands of justice and delivers those in spirit prison.

Here are the topics and prereading for Alma 54-55:

Justice separates us from God 1 Nephi 12:18, 1 Nephi 15:28-30, 2 Nephi 1:13, Helaman 5:12
- "An awful gulf, which separated the wicked from the tree of life. The justice of God did also divide the wicked from the righteous."
- "The eternal gulf of misery and endless woe."

Justice has its demands. Alma 42:21-28
- "For behold, justice exerciseth all his demands."
- "God bringeth about his great and eternal purposes, which were prepared from the foundation of the world."
- "Come and partake of the waters of life freely."

Christ's sacrifice brings mercy and satisfies the demands of justice. Alma 34:13-17
- "The intent of this last sacrifice, to bring about the bowels of mercy, which overpowereth justice."
- "…begin to call upon his holy name, that he would have mercy upon you;"

Keyword: Wine (symbolizes the blood of Christ)
- "And he took the cup, and gave thanks, and gave it to them, saying, Drink ye all of it;
- For this is my blood of the new testament, which is shed for many for the remission of sins." Matthew 26:27-28
- "And his voice shall be heard: I have trodden the wine-press alone…" D&C 133:50
- "Bless and sanctify this wine… in remembrance of the blood of thy Son." Moroni 5:2

Keyword: Sleep (symbolizes both spiritual and physical death)
- Physical death: "redemption from an endless sleep, from which sleep all men shall be awakened by the power of God when the trump shall sound." Mormon 9:13
- Spiritual death: "awake from a deep sleep, yea, even from the sleep of hell." 2 Nephi 1:13

Keyword: The Day; Work; Labor (symbolize mortal life)
Keyword: The Night; no man can work (symbolize death)
- "I must work the works of him that sent me, while it is day: the night cometh, when no man can work." John 9:4; Alma 41:5; Alma 34:32; 3 Nephi 27:33

The Armor of God, Sleep, Drunken (see Ephesians 6:14-17, 1 Thessalonians 5:6-8)
- "For they that sleep, sleep in the night; and they that be drunken are drunken in the night."
- "But let us, who are of the day, be sober, putting on the breastplate of faith and love; and for an helmet, the hope of salvation."

Satan is bound, loosed for a time, and cast into bottomless pit.
- "And he laid hold on… Satan, and bound him a thousand years… and after that he must be loosed a little season." Revelation 20:2-3,10
- "That great pit which hath been digged for the destruction of men shall be filled by those who digged it." 1 Nephi 14:3

Satisfying the Demands of Justice is like a Strategy to Free the Nephite Prisoners
Alma 54-55

As you read, see how Moroni can represent our Heavenly Father. Amalickiah can represent Satan. Similarly, Ammoron can represent the demands of justice. Moroni writes a letter to Ammoron desiring the prisoners to be set free and speaks specifically of the justice of God. In these letters, we can symbolically learn about the role of justice while Satan desires to claim God's children.

> Now these are the words which he wrote unto Ammoron, saying: Behold, I would tell you somewhat concerning *the justice of God, and the sword of his almighty wrath*, which doth hang over you except ye repent and withdraw your armies into your own lands, or the land of your possessions, which is the land of Nephi. (Alma 54:3-6 emphasis added)

Ammoron (justice) is not satisfied and demands what he believes he is due. He wants revenge for his brother. He desires what Laman and Lemuel also wanted several generations back in the Nephite account—to be the ruler (see 2 Nephi 5:3). Ammoron will never be satisfied until he can rule over the Nephites. Satan also wanted these same things in the premortal world. He had similar demands of wanting God's power and to take the kingdom (D&C 76:25-26,28).

ALMA 54:15-17,24

D&C 76:25-26,28
- WHO REBELLED AGAINST GOD
- LUCIFER... AN ANGEL OF GOD WHO WAS IN AUTHORITY
- WAS THRUST DOWN FROM THE PRESENCE OF GOD

2 NEPHI 2:29
- TO BRING YOU DOWN TO HELL

15 Now it came to pass that **Ammoron, when he had received this epistle, was angry**; and he wrote another epistle unto Moroni, and these are the words which he wrote, saying:

16 I am Ammoron, the king of the Lamanites; I am the brother of **Amalickiah whom ye have murdered**. Behold, **I will avenge his blood upon you**, yea, and I will come upon you with my armies for I fear not your threatenings.

17 For behold, **your fathers did wrong their brethren**, insomuch that **they did rob them of their right to the government** when it rightly belonged unto them.

24 And behold now, I am a bold Lamanite; behold, **this war hath been waged to avenge their wrongs**, and **to maintain and to obtain their rights to the government**; and I close my epistle to Moroni.

D&C 76:28
- SOUGHT TO TAKE THE KINGDOM

2 NEPHI 2:29
- THE DEVIL['S] POWER TO CAPTIVATE
- THAT HE MAY REIGN OVER YOU IN HIS OWN KINGDOM.

23

Nephite Event	Keywords		Premortal Event
Ammoron Demands Justice	**In order, as they appear in the text:**	**Lined up with corresponding keywords:**	**Satan Demands The Kingdom**
Alma 54:15-17,24 15 Now it came to pass that Ammoron, when he had received this epistle, was angry; and he wrote another epistle unto Moroni, and these are the words which he wrote, saying: 16 I am Ammoron, the king of the Lamanites; I am the brother of Amalickiah whom ye have murdered. Behold, I will avenge his blood upon you, yea, and I will come upon you with my armies for I fear not your threatenings. 17 For behold, your fathers did wrong their brethren, insomuch that they did rob them of their right to the government when it rightly belonged unto them. 24 And behold now, I am a bold Lamanite; behold, this war hath been waged to avenge their wrongs, and to maintain and to obtain their rights to the government; and I close my epistle to Moroni.	- Ammoron, when he had received this epistle, was angry - Amalickiah - Amalickiah whom ye have murdered - I will avenge his blood upon you - Your fathers did wrong their brethren... they did rob them of their right to the government - This war hath been waged to avenge their wrongs - To maintain and to obtain their rights to the government	- Rebelled against God - Lucifer... an angel of God who was in authority - Was thrust down from the presence of God - To bring you down to hell - Sought to take the kingdom - The devil['s] power to captivate - That he may reign over you in his own kingdom	**D&C 76:25-26,28** 25 And this we saw also, and bear record, that an angel of God who was in authority in the presence of God, who rebelled against the Only Begotten Son whom the Father loved and who was in the bosom of the Father, was thrust down from the presence of God and the Son, 26 And was called Perdition, for the heavens wept over him—he was Lucifer, a son of the morning. 28 ...we beheld Satan, that old serpent, even the devil, who rebelled against God, and sought to take the kingdom of our God and his Christ— **2 Nephi 2:29** 29 And not choose eternal death, according to the will of the flesh and the evil which is therein, which giveth the spirit of the devil power to captivate, to bring you down to hell, that he may reign over you in his own kingdom.

    This account in the Book of Mormon details how Moroni did not accept Ammoron's demand to rule over the people: "therefore Moroni resolved upon a stratagem to obtain as many prisoners of the Nephites from the Lamanites as it were possible" (see Alma 54:3). Moroni knows where the captive prisoners are being kept. Similarly, our Heavenly Father knows where the spirits are in the "space between the time of death and the resurrection... [they] are taken home to that God who gave them life" (see Alma 40:9,11).

    Consider how our Heavenly Father looked among His children for One who could go down in the form of a man, atone for mankind, satisfy the demands of justice, and set the captive spirits free. Through types and shadows, the doctrine of the condescension of God and the Savior's redemptive work is revealed from the narrative of the Book of Mormon. Moroni's strategy was to search for one of his men who looked like the Lamanites and could move freely among them, deliver the wine to the guards, and gain access to the city where the prisoners were being guarded.

Nephite Event	Keywords		Premortal Event
Moroni Searches His Men	In order, as they appear in the text:	Lined up with corresponding keywords:	The Father Asks, "Whom Shall I Send?"
Alma 55:3-5 3 Behold, I know the place where the Lamanites do guard my people whom they have taken prisoners; and as Ammoron would not grant unto me mine epistle, behold, I will give unto him according to my words; yea, I will seek death among them until they shall sue for peace. 4 And now it came to pass that when Moroni had said these words, he caused that a search should be made among his men, that perhaps he might find a man who was a descendant of Laman among them. 5 And it came to pass that they found one, whose name was Laman; and he was one of the servants of the king who was murdered by Amalickiah.	- [Moroni knows] the place where the Lamanites do guard [my] people whom they have taken prisoners - He caused that a search should be made among his men - They found one - Whose name was Laman - He was one of the servants of the king	- Concerning the state of the soul between death and the resurrection - Are taken home to that God who gave them life - And the Lord said: Whom shall I send? - One answered - The Son of Man - Here am I, send me	Alma 40:11 11 Now, concerning the state of the soul between death and the resurrection—Behold, it has been made known unto me by an angel, that the spirits of all men, as soon as they are departed from this mortal body, yea, the spirits of all men, whether they be good or evil, are taken home to that God who gave them life. Abraham 3:27 27 And the Lord said: Whom shall I send? And one answered like unto the Son of Man: Here am I, send me...

Notice how Moroni found one of his men that had the same likeness as the Lamanites. The Lamanites would have no desire to take that man captive. If he had chosen a Nephite, wartime protocol dictated the enemy camp would have taken that person captive right away. Isaiah described the Savior and His features; he would appear in a form that would not make him desirable to others (see Isaiah 53:2-3).

Moroni appoints Laman to this task. Laman then goes down with his men to follow the plan. Elder James E Faust said, "...Jesus Christ was appointed and foreordained to be our Redeemer before the world was formed. With His divine sonship, His sinless life, the shedding of His blood in the Garden of Gethsemane... He became the author of our salvation and made a perfect Atonement for all mankind."[18] The word *appointed* was also used in Helaman 1:5 in regards to Pahoran who is also a possible type of Christ (see previous chapters).

As Laman approaches the city, he meets the guards, and they hail him. Laman announces he is also a Lamanite, a prisoner of war, but had escaped from the Nephites with wine. The guards welcomed him and demanded he give them his wine.

Nephite Event	Keywords		The Condescension
They Saw Him Coming And They Hailed Him	**In order, as they appear in the text:**	**Lined up with corresponding keywords:**	**Isaiah's Description of the Savior**
Alma 55:6-8 6 Now Moroni caused that Laman and a small number of his men should go forth unto the guards who were over the Nephites. 7 Now the Nephites were guarded in the city of Gid; therefore <u>Moroni appointed Laman</u> and caused that a small number of men should go with him. 8 And when it was evening Laman went to the guards who were over the Nephites, and behold, they saw him coming and they hailed him; but he saith unto them: <u>Fear not; behold, I am a Lamanite</u>. Behold, we <u>have escaped from the Nephites</u>, and they sleep; and behold <u>we have taken of their wine and brought with us</u>.	- Moroni appointed Laman - They saw him coming and they hailed him - Fear not; behold, I am a Lamanite - Have escaped from the Nephites - We have taken of their wine and brought with us	- Jesus Christ was appointed and foreordained to be our Redeemer - He hath no form nor comeliness - When we shall see him there is no beauty that we should desire him - A man of sorrows, and acquainted with grief - With… the shedding of His blood	**Isaiah 53:2-3** 2 For he shall grow up before him as a tender plant, and as a root out of dry ground; <u>he hath no form nor comeliness</u>; and <u>when we shall see him there is no beauty that we should desire him</u>. 3 He is despised and rejected of men; <u>a man of sorrows, and acquainted with grief</u>; and we hid as it were our faces from him; he was despised, and we esteemed him not. **James E Faust, "The Atonement: our Greatest Hope" November Liahona, 2001** <u>Jesus Christ was appointed and foreordained to be our Redeemer</u> before the world was formed. <u>With</u> His divine sonship, His sinless life, <u>the shedding of His blood</u> in the Garden of Gethsemane

Keep the keyword wine in mind as this event of the Book of Mormon testifies of Christ. During the last supper Jesus "took the cup, and gave thanks, and gave it to [His disciples], saying, Drink ye all of it; For this is my blood of the new testament, which is shed for many for the remission of sins" (see Matthew 26:27-28). The Lamanite guards did not just have one drink but drank all of the wine freely until they were merry, drunken, and asleep. Alma's testimony of our ability to partake of the power of Christ's grace gives us another connected keyword: freely. He expressed, "Come and partake of the waters of life freely" (see Alma 42:27).

In the scriptural narrative, the law of justice is anthropomorphized in a sense. It has demands. It can be satisfied through the intervention of another party. It can release those who are in its grasp. Through the Savior's act of atonement, His compassion, mercy, and agony allowed Him to finish His Father's preparations and satisfy the demands of justice (see D&C 19:19).

Nephite Event	Keywords		The Atonement
Laman Offers Wine, Satisfies the Guards of the Prison	**In order, as they appear in the text:**	**Lined up with corresponding keywords:**	**Christ Offers His Blood, Satisfies the Demands of Justice**
Alma 55:9-14 9 Now when the Lamanites heard these words they received him with joy; and they said unto him: <u>Give us of your wine, that we may drink</u>; we are glad that ye have thus taken wine with you for we are weary. 10 But <u>Laman said unto them: Let us keep of our wine</u> till we go against the Nephites to battle. <u>But this saying only made them more desirous to drink of the wine</u>; 11 For, said they: We are weary, therefore <u>let us take of the wine</u>, and by and by we shall receive wine for our rations, <u>which will strengthen us</u> to go against the Nephites. 12 And <u>Laman said unto them: You may do according to your desires</u>. 13 And it came to pass that <u>they did take of the wine freely</u>; and <u>it was pleasant to their taste, therefore they took of it more freely</u>; and <u>it was strong, having been prepared in its strength</u>. 14 And it came to pass <u>they did drink and were merry, and by and by they were all drunken</u>.	- Give us of your wine, that we may drink - Laman said unto them: Let us keep of our wine - But this saying only made them more desirous to drink of the wine - Let us take of the wine - Which will strengthen us - Laman said... You may do according to your desires - They did take of the wine freely - It was pleasant to their taste - Therefore they took of it more freely - [The wine] was strong, having been prepared in its strength - They did drink and were merry - And by and by they were all drunken	- The demands of justice - Saying, Father, if thou be willing, remove this cup from me - The demands of justice - Strengthening him - Being filled with compassion towards the children of men; standing betwixt them and justice - Nevertheless not my will, but thine, be done - Partake of the waters of life freely - Being in an agony - Being justified freely by his grace - The atonement which was prepared from the foundation of the world - His sweat was... great drops of blood falling down to the ground - Having redeemed them, and satisfied the demands of justice	**Mosiah 4:7** 7 I say, that this is the man who receiveth salvation, through <u>the atonement which was prepared from the foundation of the world</u> for all mankind… **Mosiah 15:9** 9 Having ascended into heaven, having the bowels of mercy; <u>being filled with compassion towards the children of men; standing betwixt them and justice</u>; having broken the bands of death, taken upon himself their iniquity and their transgressions, <u>having redeemed them, and satisfied the demands of justice</u>. **Romans 3:24** 24 <u>Being justified freely by his grace</u> through the redemption that is in Christ Jesus: **Luke 22:42-44** 42 Saying, <u>Father, if thou be willing, remove this cup from me</u>: <u>nevertheless not my will, but thine, be done</u>. 43 And there appeared an angel unto him from heaven, <u>strengthening him</u>. 44 And <u>being in an agony</u> he prayed more earnestly: and <u>his sweat was as it were great drops of blood falling down to the ground</u>. **Alma 42:27** Therefore, O my son, whosoever will come may come and <u>partake of the waters of life freely</u>

To some readers, this wartime account simply outlines the strategy of Moroni to outmaneuver the Lamanite army. Examining this narrative through a lens seeking symbols of the plan of salvation, you can compare the willingness of Laman to risk himself to free the prisoners as a type of Christ satisfying the demands of justice. Laman, as a type of Christ, allows the prison doors to be opened for the Nephites. Then, just as Christ returned to His Father (John 20:17, Alma 55:15), Laman returned to Moroni and reported that everything went according to plan. Before you continue reading, identify a few more keywords that can reveal how the gospel is preached to those who are dead.

The keywords of *day* and *night* help us identify the continuation of the plan of salvation in Alma 55. Jesus said, "I must work the works of him that sent me, while it is day: the night cometh, when no man can work." John 9:4 In the scriptures, a solar day can typify our mortal life. Conversely, our existence after death is often equated with the night. Even though our bodies are at rest while we sleep, we still live. Even after our physical death, our spirits will likewise live.

Once Jesus completed His atoning sacrifice, He had power to go into the spirit world and liberate the captive spirits (see D&C 138). 1 Thessalonians 5:5-6 explains how we (of the day) who have the gospel can still help those (of the night) who do not have the gospel. An additional symbol would be the armor of God (Ephesians 6:14-17) which can also connect to Alma 55:15-19,22-23.

Nephite Event	Keywords		Spirit World Event
Moroni Arms the Prisoners	**In order, as they appear in the text:**	**Lined up with corresponding keywords:**	**Christ Redeems the Dead**
Alma 55:15-19,22-23 15 And now when Laman and his men saw that they were all drunken, and were in a deep sleep, they returned to Moroni and told him all the things that had happened. 16 And now this was according to the design of Moroni. And Moroni had prepared his men with weapons of war; and he went to the city Gid, while the Lamanites were in a deep sleep and drunken, and cast in weapons of war unto the prisoners, insomuch that they were all armed;	- When Laman and his men saw that they were all drunken, and were in a deep sleep - Returned to Moroni and told him all the things that had happened. This was according to the design of Moroni. And Moroni had prepared his men with weapons of war - While the Lamanites were in a deep sleep and drunken	- Let us not sleep, as do others; but let us watch and be sober - It is finished - Father, into thy hands I commend my spirit: - Let us, who are of the day, be sober, putting on the breastplate of faith and love; and for an helmet, the hope of salvation - They that be drunken are drunken in the night	**1 Thessalonians 5:6-8** 6 Therefore let us not sleep, as do others; but let us watch and be sober. 7 For they that sleep sleep in the night; and they that be drunken are drunken in the night. 8 But let us, who are of the day, be sober, putting on the breastplate of faith and love; and for an helmet, the hope of salvation. **John 19:30** 30 When Jesus therefore had received the vinegar, he said, It is finished:

17 Yea, even to their women, and all those of their children, as many as were able to use a weapon of war, when Moroni had armed all those prisoners; and all those things were done in a profound silence. 18 But had they awakened the Lamanites, behold they were drunken and the Nephites could have slain them. 19 But behold, this was not the desire of Moroni; he did not delight in murder or bloodshed, but he delighted in the saving of his people from destruction; and for this cause he might not bring upon him injustice, he would not fall upon the Lamanites and destroy them in their drunkenness. 22 Now behold this was done in the night-time, so that when the Lamanites awoke in the morning they beheld that they were surrounded by the Nephites without, and that their prisoners were armed within. 23 And thus they saw that the Nephites had power over them; and in these circumstances they found that it was not expedient that they should fight with the Nephites; therefore their chief captains demanded their weapons of war, and they brought them forth and cast them at the feet of the Nephites, pleading for mercy	- Cast in weapons of war unto the prisoners, insomuch that they were all armed - Had armed all those prisoners - All those things were done in a profound silence - He delighted in the saving of his people... and for this cause he might not bring upon him injustice, he would not... destroy them in their drunkenness - This was done in the night-time - When the Lamanites awoke in the morning they beheld that they were surrounded by the Nephites without, and that their prisoners were armed within - Their chief captains demanded their weapons of war, and they brought them forth and cast them at the feet of the Nephites, pleading for mercy	- Loins girt about with truth - The breastplate of righteousness/faith/love - Feet shod... the gospel of peace - The shield of faith - The helmet of salvation - The sword of the Spirit, which is the word of God - The dead... go down into silence - Having redeemed them, and satisfied the demands of justice - They that sleep, sleep in the night - Standing betwixt them and justice; having broken the bands of death - Having the bowels of mercy; being filled with compassion - Having redeemed them, and satisfied the demands of justic	**Luke 23:46** 46 And when Jesus had cried with a loud voice, he said, Father, <u>into thy hands I commend my spirit</u>: **Ephesians 6:14-17** 14 Stand therefore, having your <u>loins girt about with truth</u>, and having on <u>the breastplate of righteousness</u>; 15 And your <u>feet shod</u> with the preparation of <u>the gospel of peace</u>; 16 Above all, taking <u>the shield of faith</u>, wherewith ye shall be able to quench all the fiery darts of the wicked. 17 And take <u>the helmet of salvation</u>, and <u>the sword of the Spirit, which is the word of God</u>: **Psalms 115:17** <u>The dead</u> praise not the Lord, neither any that <u>go down into silence</u>. **Mosiah 15:9** 9 Having ascended into heaven, <u>having the bowels of mercy; being filled with compassion towards the children of men; standing betwixt them and justice; having broken the bands of death</u>, taken upon himself their iniquity and their transgressions, <u>having redeemed them, and satisfied the demands of justic</u>.

Compare Alma 55:20,24 to Doctrine and Covenants 138:30-31. This section details President Joseph F. Smith's record of his vision of the redemption of the dead. A side-by-side comparison reveals the gospel being preached to those in prison.

Nephite Event	Keywords		Spirit World Event
Moroni Caused All Prisoners Should Be Liberated	**In order, as they appear in the text:**	**Lined up with corresponding keywords:**	**Christ Proclaims Liberty to the Captives**
Alma 55:20 20 But he had obtained his desires; for he had armed those prisoners of the Nephites who were within the wall of the city, and had given them power to gain possession of those parts which were within the walls. **Alma 55:24** 24 Now behold, this was the desire of Moroni. He took them prisoners of war, and took possession of the city, and caused that all the prisoners should be liberated, who were Nephites; and they did join the army of Moroni, and were a great strength to his army.	- Obtained his desires - He had armed those prisoners - Given them power - To gain possession of those parts which were within the walls - This was the desire… He… took possession of the city - Caused that all the prisoners should be liberated - They did join the army… and were a great strength to his army	-He… appointed messengers - The chosen messengers went forth - Clothed with power and authority - To… carry the light of the gospel to them that were in darkness - Thus was the gospel preached to the dead - Proclaim liberty to the captives who were bound - He organized his forces	**D&C 138:30-31** 30 But behold, from among the righteous, he organized his forces and appointed messengers, clothed with power and authority, and commissioned them to go forth and carry the light of the gospel to them that were in darkness, even to all the spirits of men; and thus was the gospel preached to the dead. 31 And the chosen messengers went forth to declare the acceptable day of the Lord and proclaim liberty to the captives who were bound, even unto all who would repent of their sins and receive the gospel.

After God's children are redeemed, justice satisfied, and the spirits liberated from prison, there are still additional elements of the plan of salvation that will follow. Satan will be bound for a time and eventually cast out to that pit that he prepared himself. Continue the narrative in the Book of Mormon account. Watch how Moroni deals with the Lamanites and where they eventually end up at the end of the year.

Nephite Event	Keywords		Second Coming
Lamanite prisoners, they break loose for a time, locked in their strongholds	**In order, as they appear in the text:**	**Lined up with corresponding keywords:**	**Satan Bound for a time, loosed, and then locked away**
Alma 55: 25-26, 29-31, 33-35 25 And it came to pass that he did cause the Lamanites, whom he had taken prisoners, that they should commence a labor in strengthening the fortifications round about the city Gid. 26 And it came to pass that when he had fortified the city Gid, according to his desires, he caused that his prisoners should be taken to the city Bountiful; and he also guarded that city with an exceedingly strong force. 29 Many times did the Lamanites attempt to encircle them about by night, but in these attempts they did lose many prisoners. 30 And many times did they attempt to administer of their wine to the Nephites, that they might destroy them with poison or with drunkenness. 31 But behold, the Nephites were not slow to remember the Lord their God in this their time of affliction. They could not be taken in their snares; yea, they would not partake of their wine, save they had first given to some of the Lamanite prisoners. 33 And now it came to pass that it was expedient for Moroni to make preparations to attack the city Morianton; for behold, the Lamanites had, by their labors, fortified the city Morianton until it had become an exceeding stronghold. 34 And they were continually bringing new forces into that city, and also new supplies of provisions. 35 And thus ended the twenty and ninth year of the reign of the judges over the people of Nephi.	- The Lamanites, whom he had taken prisoners - His prisoners should be taken to the city Bountiful; - The Lamanites attempt to encircle them about by night, but in these attempts they did lose many prisoners - The Nephites were not slow to remember the Lord their God in this their time of affliction. They could not be taken in their snare - The Lamanites had, by their labors, fortified the city Morianton - They were continually bringing new forces into that city - And thus ended the twenty and ninth year	- Having the key of the bottomless pit - Laid hold on the dragon... the Devil, and Satan, and bound him - Cast him into the bottomless pit, and shut him up - After that he must be loosed a little season - He should deceive the nations no more - There is a place prepared, yea, even that awful hell - The bottomless pit - The devil is the preparator of it - That great pit which hath been digged for the destruction of men shall be filled by those who digged it - The devil is the preparator of it - The final state... cast out because of that justice - And shall be tormented day and night for ever and ever	**Revelation 20:2-3,10** 2 And he laid hold on the dragon, that old serpent, which is the Devil, and Satan, and bound him a thousand years, 3 And cast him into the bottomless pit, and shut him up, and set a seal upon him, that he should deceive the nations no more, till the thousand years should be fulfilled: and after that he must be loosed a little season. 10 And the devil that deceived them was cast into the lake of fire and brimstone, where the beast and the false prophet are, and shall be tormented day and night for ever and ever. **1 Nephi 14:3** 3 ...yea, that great pit which hath been digged for the destruction of men shall be filled by those who digged it **1 Nephi 15:35** And there is a place prepared, yea, even that awful hell of which I have spoken, and the devil is the preparator of it; wherefore the final state of the souls of men is to dwell in the kingdom of God, or to be cast out because of that justice of which I have spoken.

The Book of Mormon narrative reveals the plan of salvation. It testifies of Christ and does so on every page. As you come across a chapter that may not explicitly speak of Christ and His gospel, ask yourself, "Through these events of the Book of Mormon, how am I being instructed in the plan of salvation?" Symbolic learning can help reveal an answer to you. Reflecting on this important question can aid you even if you don't have extended time to study the scriptures. When you are sitting somewhere with only a few minutes to read, like in a chapel before a meeting begins, outside the bishop's (or doctor's) office, or waiting for a friend to arrive, you can open to any page in the Book of Mormon and ask that same question. Even a brief study moment can aid you in learning the plan of salvation and taking a step closer to Christ.

*"If they saw our day and chose those things which would be of greatest worth
to us, is not that how we should study the Book of Mormon?
We should constantly ask ourselves,
'Why did the Lord inspire Mormon (or Moroni or Alma)
to include that in his record? What lesson can I learn from that
to help me live in this day and age?"*
- Ezra Taft Benson

4

MORTAL LIFE: DEFENDING AND PROTECTING OUR HOMES

Captain Moroni is introduced to students of the Book of Mormon in Alma 43-44. The context of this portion of the Nephite record is focused on the wars and conflicts engulfing their society. Jesus Christ is rarely mentioned in this section of scripture. Nevertheless, as you study this portion of the Book of Mormon look for what you can learn About a key part of the plan of salvation—mortal life. Through Captain Moroni's physical battle with the Lamanites, you will learn how to navigate spiritual battles against the devil and his angels.

As you study the prereading section, write down what you think the keywords could be that cue your mind to elements of the plan of salvation. Ponder the verses. As you study in Alma, go back and reread verses to discover additional connections with other scriptures. Write down the insights that come to you as you frame your study with a goal to learn and apply the principles available in these sacred records. You can find true joy as you approach your gospel study with a hunger for additional truth and spiritual power.

A Worksheet: Alma 43-44

Pre-reading for Pondering and Identifying Keywords:

Alma 43:1-54   Alma 44:1-9   Ephesians 6:11-18   Revelations 20:2
James 4:7   2 Nephi 2:13 Alma 41:10

As you study the chapters describing the Nephite conflicts, types and shadows can provide insights into both sides of the war. On one side, Jesus Christ is supporting parents who seek to protect their family from the opposing side of Satan and his followers. You will see the desires and tactics employed by both sides. You gain insight into who will be the victor and why. President Gordon B. Hinckley declared,

> "The issue then was free agency as it is today. Then, as now, choices had to be made. 'And there was war in heaven: Michael and his angels fought against the dragon; and the dragon fought and his angels, And prevailed not; neither was their place found any more in heaven.' That ancient struggle continues, the unrelenting battle that comes of free agency. Some, unfortunately, choose the wrong. But many, so many, choose the right, including so very many of our choice young men and young women. They deserve and need our gratitude. They need our encouragement. They need the kind of examples that we can become before them."[9]

As you study, the Book of Mormon can show you how to fortify your own homes against the wiles of the devil. This can give you strength to valiantly endure the present portion of the plan of salvation you are living in—mortality.

Roles: Alma 43:5,16,23	*Weapons of Each:*
Lucifer: _____ _____	Lucifer's weapons and clothing: Alma 43:20–21 _____
Christ/Parents: _____	
Prophets: <u>Spies, Alma</u>	
What is the role of a spy? _____	
	What can you attack with, and what can you defend with? _____
How is the role of a spy similar to the role of a prophet? _____	
Intention of Each: Alma 43:6–8,4,9,24	Parent's weapons and clothing: Alma 43:18–19; Ephesians 6:11–18 _____
Lucifer's desires: _____	
Parent's design for their families: _____	What can you attack with, and what can you defend with? _____
Prophets warn us of our _____	

Tactics:

Satan's tactics: Alma 43:24 _____
_____
_____
_____
_____

Parents tactics: Alma 43:29–30 _____
_____
_____
_____
_____

Is the ending predictable when you see that one army can only attack and one can attack and defend? What defense does Satan have? How do we fight against Satan and his angels? Alma 43:37–42; Ephesians 6:12; James 4:7 _____
_____
_____
_____

Inspiration, for Each Side:

Satan's motivation to his army: Alma 43:43–44; Revelations 20:2 _____
_____
_____
_____
_____

How righteous parent's inspire the family (resist the urge to flee): Alma 43:48–50 ___
_____
_____
_____
_____
_____
_____

The Reasons for Victory and Defeat:

Why parents can win: Alma 44:1–5 (how many times is the word "faith" used?); 2 Nephi 2:13, Alma 41:10 _____
_____
_____
_____
_____
_____

What Satan attributes his loss to: Alma 44:9
_____
_____
_____
_____
_____
_____

As you compare the two explanations, Notice the keywords are the same?

Shield = _____

Breastplates = _____

Swords = _____

What have you learned from this battle? ___
_____
_____
_____
_____
_____
_____
_____
_____

"...when we really take time to ponder the Plan, it is breathtaking and over-powering! Indeed, I, for one, cannot decide which creates in me the most awe—its very vastness or its intricate, individualized detail."
- Neil A. Maxwell

5

SEE YOURSELF IN THE PLAN

God's plan for His children is inclusive and individualized. It has an intricacy that weaves our personal paths together into a comprehensive conduit for all to receive His promised blessings through obedience to eternal law. God's creations are as meaningful and practical for the individual as they are for His children collectively. It is as if He fashioned the Earth just for you—and fashioned a plan for redemption specifically for you. Each day can serve as an opportunity to remember these important truths.

Always Remember Him, That You May Have His Spirit to be With You

Each sabbath day, the sacrament prayers offer members of the congregation to covenant to "always remember [Jesus Christ]" (see Moroni 4:3–5:2). Remembering Him can be hard to do within the hustle and bustle of everyday life. Perhaps hearing this repeated phrase is one reason members of the Church are to "meet together oft" to partake of the sacrament (see Moroni 6:5).

One way you can keep the Savior as an integral part of your daily life is to study how the plan of salvation is revealed in the narrative of the Book of Mormon. The scriptures are accounts of individuals, families, and communities searching to follow God and His plan for them. Sometimes they got sidetracked or stalled on their journey. They rejoiced when they received additional gospel truth, light, and direction. They participated in acts of creation. They experienced destruction as they turned from God and His laws. They were redeemed as they abandoned evil and turned to Him with faith. They faced death with courage and confidence that life would continue through the power of Jesus Christ's resurrection. They enjoyed His holy presence and felt His love personally.

You can gain spiritual power to recognize God's design for your life as you study these patterns and consider how your daily narrative includes corresponding elements of the plan of salvation. The Book of Mormon was written for our day (See Mormon 8:34–35). You can experience the same blessings of the plan of salvation experienced by the people in the scriptures. As you continue learning how the plan of salvation is revealed by the people, places, and events in the Book of Mormon, you can deepen your understanding on how the plan is revealed in the narrative of your own life.

This practice is not very mysterious. It is common for readers of all ages to extract important truth and wisdom through novels or biographies. President Dieter F. Uchtdorf characterized these works as "journey stories." He commented on notable works of fiction including The Wizard of Oz, A Christmas Carol, Journey to the West, and The Hobbit: "Don't we love these journey stories because we can see ourselves in the travelers? Their successes and failures can help us find our own way through life."[5]

Turning to fiction novels and learning courage from those characters is easy to do. Turning to biographies of notable men and women and learning from their mistakes and successes is wonderful. Turning to a book that "[came] forth by the gift and power of God"[6] to help you learn will help exponentially more as you take a similar approach to the Book of Mormon. Consider these steps as you incorporate this practice:

1. Recognize the plan of salvation in the lives of Book of Mormon peoples and their teachings.
2. Recognize the plan operating in your own life.
3. Seeking for the Holy Ghost to confirm these truths and aid you in seeing the Savior's role in the plan for God's children—in God's plan for you.

The Plan in Our Own Day-to-Day Narrative

Our own lives have many parallels to the plan of salvation. You may often hear these parallels presented in examples during General Conference addresses, gospel messages in sacrament services, Sunday School lessons, and in your own conversations with friends and family. You can fall into the trap of seeing those applications as relevant to others but not in your own life. At times, you may fail to identify the significance of certain events until long after they have occurred. Imagine if you could frame the gospel application of the everyday events of your life through the lens of the plan of salvation. Imagine if you could use seemingly mundane events as opportunities to always remember Jesus Christ and have His spirit to be with you. Elder Duane B. Gerrard of the Seventy spoke of his own experiences as an airline pilot and how the flight plans he filled out every day kept his mind on the plan of salvation. He stated:

As a recently retired airline pilot, I've filed many flight plans in my years of flying—flight plans that led me safely to my destination. Airlines also have laws, procedures, principles, and regulations. We carefully follow these strict procedures and checklists that are grouped into three specific areas. What a great and wonderful plan is the plan of salvation, which, like the many flight plans I've filed, teaches true principles to allow completion of our journey through life."[7]

Elements of the Plan of Salvation Expressed in the Book of Mormon and Our Daily Life		
Plan of Salvation element	**Event from the Book of Mormon narrative**	**Event from your daily life**
War in heaven	Amlici creates contention and desires to be king. (see Alma 2:1-4)	Before school, two siblings arguing for the front seat of the car
Leaving our heavenly home	Lehi leaves his Jerusalem home. (see 1 Nephi 2:2–4)	Departing from your home to travel to work/school each day.
The creation of the Earth	Zeniff's people till the ground in the land of Nephi (see Mosiah 9:9)	Planting and watering an herb garden on your windowsill.
Coming to Earth (our second estate)	The Jaredites traveled in barges guided by God. (see Ether 6:2–4)	Traveling alone, or with other people, and arriving at school or work.
Spiritual death	Dissenters are flattered by the words of wicked Amalickiah. (See Alma 46:5–6)	Being persuaded by a friend to lower your standards for media.
Physical death	Alma witnesses the righteous saints put to death. (see Alma 14:8–17)	Getting let-go from your job even when you were a good employee.
Redemption from spiritual death	Nephi forgave his brothers when they asked for it. (see 1 Nephi 7:20–21)	Your neighbor accepts your apology with graciousness.
Preaching the gospel in the world of spirits	Ammon frees his brothers from Prison with Lamoni's help. (see Alma 20:28)	Ministers visit the home of someone trying to repent or return to church activity.
Redemption from physical death	Lehi's family fears they will drown but God saves them and calms the storm. (see 1 Nephi 18:20–21)	Learning that you got hired at that new job; feeling of comfort from pain or grief.
Judgement	Jacob teaches about good fruit and corrupt fruit. (see Jacob 5:75)	Picking out produce at the market for your evening meal.
Eternal Life/Exaltation	Nephites and Lamanites are separated into different kingdoms. (see 2 Nephi 5:1-3, 5–6)	Returning home and spending time with your family.

Throughout this book, you have reviewed many types and shadows that reveal the plan of salvation. Is there much difference between taking a journey to the promised land or going to the store to buy groceries? Don't both events have the same ability to offer gospel applications? At times, you may get stuck in your daily life and fail to remember the Savior or seek the Holy Ghost to guide you. Yet, if you remember these types and shadows when you leave home, while at school or work, and you stay true to your covenants when you return home again, you will access more of God's power in your day. You can faithfully endure through hard times that come and rejoice in the blessings that are given. President Packer's words summarize well the need for repetitive study of the plan of salvation and finding ourselves daily in that plan:

> You will not be with your students or your own children at the time of their temptations. At those dangerous moments they must depend on their own resources. If they can locate themselves within the framework of the gospel plan, they will be immensely strengthened. The plan is worthy of repetition over and over again. Then the purpose of life, the reality of the Redeemer, and the reason for the commandments will stay with them.[19]

Just as seemingly inconsequential events in Nephite history can teach important truths about the plan of salvation, the mundane activities in your own lives can offer similar opportunities: every moment can be instructive if you allow it to call to your minds the truths of God's plan. In doing this, you will remember your Savior Jesus Christ more often and always have His spirit to be with you.

"Brethren, how can we truly understand who we are unless we know who we were and what we have the power to become? How can there be real identity without real history? How can one understand his tiny, individual plot without knowing, even a little, about Father's grand, galactic plans?"
- Neil A. Maxwell

6

THE PLAN OF SALVATION IS A KEY TO CONVERSION

The plan of salvation—also known as the plan of redemption, and the plan of happiness—is a key ingredient to enduring conversion to the gospel of Jesus Christ. The plan provides purpose, clarity, and direction for our existence. It explains to us the why behind the creation, the fall, our mortal lives, and the Atonement of Jesus Christ. God's emphasis on the plan is highlighted when He taught Adam and Eve commandments after they had left the garden. Alma reveals, "Therefore God gave unto them commandments, after having made known unto them the plan of redemption" (See Alma 12:32; Moses 6:58–68). Without the context of God's plan, commandments can seem like a group of arbitrary rules mortals are forced to follow. God wants his children to understand the "why" behind everything he does.

Understanding the plan of salvation is essential as you continue to grow in the gospel and work through the trials and tribulations that are a part of life. As you study the plan of salvation, you will also find the answers you seek and the direction you need to continue your progression and stay on the covenant path. President Oaks declared, "I share the conviction that has come to me from many letters and by reviewing many requests to return to the Church after name removal or apostasy. Many of our members do not fully understand this plan of salvation, which answers most questions about the doctrine and inspired policies of the restored Church."[4]

The Lord has provided a way for us to find the plan of salvation outlined in the recorded sermons and teachings of the prophets and through the narrative of the Book of Mormon. As the plan is revealed to us through our study, our testimonies grow, we come closer to Christ, and our conversion deepens.

A scriptural example of deep conversion is the group of Lamanites who change their name to the people of Anti-Nephi-Lehi (See Alma 23:16–17). Mormon, in his abridgment, gives the main desire of the sons of Mosiah in their mission to the Lamanites: "Therefore, this was the cause for which the sons of Mosiah had undertaken the work, that perhaps they might bring them unto repentance; that perhaps they might bring them to know of the plan of redemption" (see Alma 17:16; emphasis added). In Alma 24, the new king of the people of Anti-Nephi-Lehi expresses that Ammon and his brethren achieved their cause. The king exclaims, "And the great God has had mercy on us, and made these things known unto us that we might not perish; yea, and he has made these things known unto us beforehand, because he loveth our souls as well as he loveth our children; therefore, in his mercy he doth visit us by his angels, that the plan of salvation might be made known unto us as well as unto future generations" (see Alma 24:14; emphasis added).

As the people of Anti-Nephi-Lehi understood the plan of salvation, they were motivated to repent, live righteously, and overcome incredible odds. They were even willing to accept death at the hands of their enemies. They were able to do all of this because they understood that mortality was not the end of God's plan and that their covenants and repentance saved them from both physical and spiritual death. This understanding of the plan of salvation is explained as the king continues his address: "And now, my brethren, if our brethren seek to destroy us, behold, we will hide away our swords, yea, even we will bury them deep in the earth, that they may be kept bright, as a testimony that we have never used them, at the last day; and if our brethren destroy us, behold, we shall go to our God and shall be saved." (see Alma 24:16; emphasis added).

Mormon emphasizes that this group of Christians knew this life was not the end of existence. Mormon's inclusion of the phrase "and thus we see" twice in this verse reinforces the critical insight he hopes we will receive: "And thus we see that, when these Lamanites were brought to believe and to know the truth, they were firm, and would suffer even unto death rather than commit sin; and thus we see that they buried their weapons of peace, or they buried the weapons of war, for peace" (see Alma 24:19; emphasis added). This conversion had lasting impact to the people and their posterity.

A Generational Timeline of the Firmness of Converted Lamanites

136 Years of The Influence of The Plan of Salvation		
Time	People	Verse
90-77 BC	Anti-Nephi-Lehi's	"And as sure as the Lord liveth, so sure as many as believed, or as many as were brought to the knowledge of the truth, through the preaching of Ammon and his brethren... *as many of the Lamanites as believed in their preaching, and were converted unto the Lord, never did fall away.*" (Alma 23:6; emphasis added)
		"that the plan of salvation might be made known unto us *as well as unto future generations*" (Alma 24:14; emphasis added)

65-64 BC	Sons of Helaman	"*Now they never had fought, yet they did not fear death;* and they did think more upon the liberty of their fathers than they did upon their lives; yea, they had been taught by their mothers, that if they did not doubt, God would deliver them." (Alma 56:47–48; emphasis added)
6 BC	Before Christ's Birth	"And behold, ye do know of yourselves, for ye have witnessed it, that as many of them as are brought to the knowledge of the truth… are *firm and steadfast in the faith*, and in the thing wherewith they have been made free…; yea, *ye can see that they fear to sin—for behold they will suffer themselves that they be trodden down and slain by their enemies, and will not lift their swords against them, and this because of their faith in Christ*." (Helaman 15:7–9; emphasis added)
AD 26-30	After Christ's Birth	"in the thirtieth year the church was broken up in all the land save it were among a few of the Lamanites who were converted unto the true faith; and they would not depart from it, for t*hey were firm, and steadfast, and immovable, willing with all diligence to keep the commandments of the Lord*." (3 Nephi 6:14; emphasis added)
AD 34-35	At the Sign of Christ's Death	"And it was *the more righteous part of the people who were saved*, and it was they who received the prophets and stoned them not; and it was they who had not shed the blood of the saints, who were spared." (3 Nephi 10:12; emphasis added)
AD 35	After Christ's Visit	"And it came to pass in the thirty and sixth year, *the people were all converted unto the Lord, upon all the face of the land, both Nephites and Lamanites*, and there were no contentions and disputations among them, and every man did deal justly one with another." (4 Nephi 1:2; emphasis added)

Notice over a full century of righteous living was produced by a people with a firm grasp of the truths offered through the plan of salvation. Even within a period of intense wickedness of the surrounding society, the people of God prepared themselves to receive great manifestations and the personal ministry of Jesus Christ.

As you understand the plan of salvation, you can also be blessed with a deeper personal conversion. You will be able to see yourself in the plan and be firm—overcoming your own trials in this modern life by following the examples of this ancient text. You can then pass on that knowledge to your children and bless future generations. You can use the side-by-side technique of studying a parable to see types and shadows of the plan of salvation in the narrative of the Book of Mormon.

Please heed the constant call from our prophets and apostles to read and reread the Book of Mormon, so you can come unto Christ and embed the plan of salvation deeper into your hearts and the hearts of your children.

References

PREFACE:

1. Opening Quote: Ezra Taft Benson "The Book of Mormon and the Doctrine and Covenants" Liahona, May 1987
2. Smith, History of the Church, 6:50. See also Times and Seasons 4, no. 21 (September 15, 1843): 331-32
3. Ezra Taft Benson "The Book of Mormon and the Doctrine and Covenants" Liahona, May 1987

CHAPTER 1: REVEALING THE PLAN OF SALVATION

1. Opening quote: Neil A Maxwell, "God Will Yet Reveal", Liahona November, 1986
2. See Bible Dictionary, Mystery p.736
3. 1 Corinthians 2:9-12
4. Jarom 1:2
5. 2 Nephi 2:14-29
6. Words of Mormon 1:7
7. Abraham 3:22-28
8. Doctrine and Covenants 29:36-37
9. Abraham 3:27
10. Revelation 13:8
11. Abraham 3:27-28
12. Doctrine and Covenants 29:36-37
13. Revelation 12:4,7-11
14. Moses 4:3
15. Doctrine and Covenants 29:36-37
16. Doctrine and Covenants 29:36-39
17. Helaman 1:1-12
18. Mormon 3:20
19. Abraham 3:27
20. Abraham 3:28
21. Revelation 12:4,7-11
22. Doctrine and Covenants 29:36
23. Abraham 3:27-28
24. Moses 4:3
25. Revelation 13:8
26. 3 Nephi 27:14
27. Doctrine and Covenants 29:37
28. LeGrand Richards "The Simplicity in Christ" October Liahona 1976
29. Alma 32:28
30. Doctrine and Covenants 27:5

CHAPTER 2: PARABLES, TYPES, AND SHADOWS

1. Opening quote: Bible Dictionary: Parable
2. Matthew 13:10-11
3. Bible Dictionary: Parable
4. Matthew 13:31-32,44, 47
5. Helaman 1:1-12
6. John 14:26
7. Joseph Smith, The King Follett Sermon, Teachings, 350–52
8. Alma 30:44
9. 1 Nephi 8:1
10. 1 Nephi 17:4,6,8,10,36
11. 1 Nephi 18:1-2,4-6, 8
12. Genesis 1:10, 12
13. Abraham 3:24
14. Dallin H. Oaks, "The Great Plan of Happiness" Liahona, Nov 1993
15. Mosiah 9:6-9
16. Mosiah 9:5,10-11
17. Mosiah 10:3-5
18. Genesis 1:28
19. Genesis 2:5
20. Genesis 3:6-7
21. 2 Nephi 28:19,21-22
22. Russell M. Nelson, "The Creation," Liahona, May 2000
23. Plan of Salvation Circular layout used with permission

CHAPTER 3: THIS PATTERN TESTIFIES OF CHRIST

1. Opening quote: Russell M. Nelson "Embrace the Future with Faith" Liahona November 2020
2. Susan Easton Black, Finding Christ through the Book of Mormon [1987], 16-18
3. 1 Nephi 12:18
4. 1 Nephi 15:28-30
5. 2 Nephi 1:13
6. Helaman 5:12
7. Alma 42:21-28
8. Alma 34:13-17
9. Alma 54:3-6
10. 2 Nephi 5:3
11. D&C 76:25-26,28
12. 2 Nephi 2:29
13. Alma 54:3
14. Alma 40:9,11
15. Alma 40:11
16. Abraham 3:27
17. Isaiah 53:2-3
18. James E Faust,"The Atonement: our Greatest Hope" November Liahona, 2001
19. Isaiah 53:2-3
20. Matthew 26:27-28

21. Alma 42:27
22. D&C 19:19
23. Mosiah 4:7
24. Mosiah 15:9
25. Romans 3:24
26. Luke 22:42-44
27. Alma 42:27
28. John 20:17
29. Alma 55:15
30. John 9:4
31. D&C 138
32. 1 Thessalonians 5:5-6
33. Ephesians 6:14-17
34. Alma 55:15-19,22-23
35. 1 Thessalonians 5:6-8
36. John 19:30
37. Luke 23:46
38. Ephesians 6:14-17
39. Psalms 115:17
40. Mosiah 15:9
41. Alma 55:20,24
42. Doctrine and Covenants 138:30-31
43. Revelation 20:2-3,10
44. 1 Nephi 14:3
45. 1 Nephi 15:35

CHAPTER 4: MORTAL LIFE: DEFENDING AND PROTECTING OUR HOMES
1. Opening quote: Ezra Taft Benson "The Book of Mormon—Keystone of Our Religion" November Liahona, 1986
2. Alma 43:1-54
3. Alma 44:1-9
4. Ephesians 6:11-18
5. Revelations 20:2
6. James 4:7
7. 2 Nephi 2:13
8. Alma 41:10
9. Gordon B. Hinckley, "We Have a Work to Do" Liahona, May 1995

CHAPTER 5: SEEING YOURSELF IN THE PLAN
1. Opening quote: Neal A Maxwell, "Thanks Be To God," Liahona July, 1982
2. Moroni 4:3–5:2
3. Moroni 6:5
4. Mormon 8:34–35
5. Dieter F. Uchtdorf "Your Wonderful Journey Home" Liahona, April 2013
6. See Title Page of the Book of Mormon
7. Duane B. Gerrard "The Plan of Salvation: A Flight Plan for Life" November Liahona, 1997
8. Alma 2:1-4

9. 1 Nephi 2:2–4
10. Mosiah 9:9
11. Ether 6:2–4
12. Alma 46:5–6
13. Alma 14:8–17
14. 1 Nephi 7:20–21
15. Alma 20:28
16. 1 Nephi 18:20–21
17. Jacob 5:75
18. 2 Nephi 5:1-3, 5–6
19. The Great Plan of Happiness, Elder Boyd K. Packer, Address to religious educators at a symposium on the Doctrine and Covenants and Church history, Brigham Young University, 10 August 1993

CHAPTER 6: THE PLAN OF SALVATION IS A KEY TO CONVERSION

1. Opening quote: Neal A. Maxwell "Called and Prepared from the Foundation of the World" Liahona April 1986
2. See Alma 12:32
3. Moses 6:58–68
4. Dallin H. Oaks, "The Great Plan" Liahona May, 2020
5. See Alma 23:16–17
6. Alma 17:16
7. Alma 24:14
8. Alma 24:16
9. Alma 24:19
10. Alma 23:6
11. Alma 24:14
12. Alma 56:47–48
13. Helaman 15:7–9
14. 3 Nephi 6:14
15. 3 Nephi 10:12
16. 4 Nephi 1:2

About the Author

Cameron is a licensed clinical social worker helping people overcome their mental health challenges. He is a believer in simple, daily, spiritual study that includes pondering.

He lives in Utah with his wife and three children.

Learn more at cameron-r-armstrong.com

**Other Books
By
Cameron Reid Armstrong**

You don't have to like speaking in church, but you don't have to be afraid of it either.

Discover the mindsets and principles for writing and giving a good talk designed for members of the Church of Jesus Christ of Latter-day Saints; applying principles of public speaking to our Sacrament Services. Cameron uses personal examples of those principles in simple and applicable ways.

This book will raise the confidence of your skills, while refining your mindset about public speaking.

- Crafting examples that focus on the message
- Effectively using assigned conference talks
- Avoiding disclaimers with confidence
- Researching and building an outline
- Testifying with less storytelling
- How to handle your emotions
- Advice for high councilors
- Mission Preparation

Available on Amazon KDP

Made in United States
Troutdale, OR
06/18/2025